just THE JOB

Working with the Past

*Also published in the **Just the Job!** series:*

- Art & Design
- Beauty, Hairdressing & Fashion
- Care & Community
- Construction & Architecture
- Consumer & Home Services
- Engineering
- Finance & Financial Services
- Horticulture, Forestry & Farming
- Hospitality, Food, Travel & Tourism
- In Uniform
- Information & The Written Word
- Land & The Environment
- Law & Order
- Leisure, Sport & Entertainment
- Management, Marketing & PR
- Manufacturing & Production
- Medicine & Health
- Motor Vehicles & Transport
- Nursing & Therapies
- Office & Administrative Work
- Scientific Work
- Selling, Retailing & Distribution
- Teaching
- Telecommunications, Film & Video
- Working with Animals
- Working with your Hands

just THE JOB
Working with the Past

Lifetime Careers
WILTSHIRE

Hodder & Stoughton
A MEMBER OF THE HODDER HEADLINE GROUP

Just the Job! draws directly on the CLIPS careers information database developed and maintained by Lifetime Careers Wiltshire and used by almost every careers service in the UK. The database is revised annually using a rigorous update schedule and incorporates material collated through desk/telephone research and information provided by all the professional bodies, institutions and training bodies with responsibility for course accreditation and promotion of each career area.

ISBN 0 340 68779 7
First published 1997

Impression number	10	9	8	7	6	5	4	3	2	1
Year			2002	2001	2000	1999	1998	1997		

Copyright © 1997 Lifetime Careers Wiltshire Ltd

All rights reserved. No part of this publication may be reproduced or transmitted in any form or by any means, electronic or mechanical, including photocopy, recording or any information storage and retrieval system, without permission in writing from the publisher or under licence from the Copyright Licensing Agency Ltd. Further details of such licences (for reprographic reproduction) may be obtained from the Copyright Licensing Agency Ltd, 90 Tottenham Court Road, London W1P 9HE.

Printed in Great Britain for Hodder & Stoughton Educational, the educational publishing division of Hodder Headline Plc, 338 Euston Road, London NW1 3BH, by Cox & Wyman Ltd, Reading, Berkshire.

just THE JOB

CONTENTS

Introduction	9
Archaeologist	14
Archivist	20
Heraldry & genealogy	24
Heritage jobs	28
Preserving and restoring. Recording and researching. Administration. Tourism, marketing and publicity. Service jobs. Education/information officer.	
Museum work	35
Curator. Conservation staff. Design staff, modelmakers, taxidermists, photographers, etc. Educational staff.	
Careers in art galleries	44
Working in antiques	49
Restoring works of art	54
Restorer. Conservator.	
Working in libraries & information services	59
Exhibition & conference organising	69
Display, exhibition & interior design	73
Theatre & TV work	77
Horologist	85
For further information	88

JUST THE JOB!

The *Just the Job!* series ranges over the entire spectrum of occupations and is intended to generate job ideas and stretch horizons of interest and possibility, allowing you to explore families of jobs for which you might have appropriate ability and aptitude. Each *Just the Job!* book looks in detail at a popular area or type of work, covering:

- ways into work;
- essential qualifications;
- educational and training options;
- working conditions;
- progression routes;
- potential career portfolios.

The information given in *Just the Job!* books is detailed and carefully researched. Obvious bias is excluded to give an even-handed picture of the opportunities available, and course details and entry requirements are positively checked in an annual update cycle by a team of careers information specialists. The text is written in approachable, plain English, with a minimum of technical terms.

In Britain today, there is no longer the expectation of a career for life, but support has increased for life-long learning and the acquisition of skills which will help young and old to make sideways career moves – perhaps several times during a working life – as well as moving into work carrying higher levels of responsibility and reward. *Just the Job!* invites you to select an appropriate direction for your *own* career progression.

Educational and vocational qualifications

A level – Advanced level of the General Certificate of Education
AS level – Advanced Supplementary level of the General Certificate of Education (equivalent to half an A level)
BTEC – Business and Technology Education Council: awards qualifications such as BTEC First, BTEC National Certificate/Diploma, etc
GCSE – General Certificate of Secondary Education
GNVQ/GSVQs – General National Vocational Qualification/General Scottish Vocational Qualification: awarded at Foundation, Intermediate and Advanced levels by BTEC, City & Guilds, Royal Society of Arts and the Scottish Qualifications Authority (SQA)
HND/C – BTEC Higher National Diploma/Certificate
International Baccalaureate – recognised by all UK universities as equivalent to a minimum of two A levels
NVQ/SVQs – National/Scottish Vocational Qualifications
SCE – Scottish Certificate of Education, at **Standard** Grade (equate directly with GCSEs: grades 1–3 in SCEs at Standard Grade are equivalent to GCSE grades A–C) and **Higher** Grade (equate with the academic level attained after one year of a two-year A level course: three to five Higher Grades are broadly equivalent to two to four A levels at grades A–E)

Vocational work-based credits	NVQ/SVQ level 1	NVQ/SVQ level 2	NVQ/SVQ level 3	NVQ/SVQ level 4
Vocational qualifications: *a mix of theory and practice*	Foundation GNVQ/GSVQ; BTEC First	Intermediate GNVQ/GSVQ	Advanced GNVQ/GSVQ; BTEC National Diploma/Certificate	BTEC Higher National Diploma/Certificate
Educational qualifications	GCSE/SCE Standard Grade pass grades	GCSE grades A–C; SCE Standard Grade levels 1–3	Two A levels; four Scottish Highers; Baccalaureate	University degree

INTRODUCTION

People who are keen on history often wonder what use they could make of this interest in terms of their career. In fact, the study of history trains you to find out the reasons underlying past events, using methods you can apply in many other work areas, such as law and the Civil Service. Some careers call for a degree; others make use of A level or GCSE-level knowledge of history.

As an examination subject, history is always acceptable in fulfilling qualification requirements for numbers of GCSE passes, sometimes even being used as an alternative to an exam pass in English, because of the amount of written work involved.

Skills you learn in history

- the skills of investigation – how to collect evidence; how to assess its reliability and its relevance, and how to detect bias;
- how to put yourself in the shoes of a particular person in a particular situation;
- how to analyse a situation, establishing cause and effect;
- how to present all the information you have gathered;
- how to argue a case.

Skills such as these are applicable in lots of occupations.

What subjects can you combine with history?

If you are thinking of taking history at GCSE or A level, or equivalent, you may be wondering what subjects to combine it with. There are a lot of subjects which go well with history, depending to some extent on what your particular interests are, but the following are specially useful:

Modern and classical languages – a knowledge of one or more languages enables you to read source material in the original language, if you are studying foreign, ancient or medieval history, for instance. Languages are felt to be desirable by a number of universities offering history degrees. Modern languages will also be an asset in many careers, especially with the opening up of opportunities in Europe.

Economics and geography – both combine well with history in giving background knowledge. It is possible to become a specialist in economic history.

Mathematics and computing – these can be useful subjects as historians use the techniques of maths and computing for analysing data (e.g. searches through old records, distribution data, etc).

Science subjects – these, particularly chemistry, are useful to would-be archaeologists and conservators.

English literature – can provide the historian with a good deal of background information and context, enhancing a general understanding of a period.

Leisure & Tourism, **Information Technology**, **Science** or **Business GNVQs** can all be usefully combined with history for similar reasons to those above.

At *degree* level, besides studying history on its own, you can combine it with many other subjects, perhaps one chosen from the above list, or from other possibilities such as law, politics, nautical studies, art, music, sociology and education. As a subject in its own right, it is possible to take a very broad degree in history. Alternatively, you can specialise in the history of particular countries or particular periods, or in areas such as economic history, intellectual history, philosophy of history, and so on. The various degree course handbooks will show you the range available.

Three main ways of 'using' history

- Work where it is important or useful to have a knowledge of historical events, in order to understand current affairs, for example:
  Broadcasting
  Civil Service (some aspects)
  Diplomatic Service
  European Commission
  Journalism
  Local government (some aspects)
  Politics
  Trade union work
- Work which can make good use of the research, investigatory and report-writing techniques learned in studying history, for example:
  Civil Service
  Information work
  Journalism
  Law
  Librarianship
  Management
  Patent agency
  Police work
  Publishing
- Work where you need a knowledge of the past or of historical objects, for example:
  Academic library work
  Antiquarian bookbinding
  Antiquarian bookselling
  Antiques
  Archaeology (includes ancient monument inspection)

Architecture
Archive work
Conservation/natural history
Heraldry/genealogy
Heritage jobs
Interior design
Museum work
Picture restoring
Taxidermy
Teaching history
Theatre/TV costumes, props, etc
Town and country planning
TV/radio programme research

Many of the occupations in the third group, where a knowledge of history or historical objects is important, are competitive to enter. These jobs are mostly for graduates in history or archaeology, or in other appropriate specialist subjects, though in some there are opportunities for people with lower qualifications.

Working as a historian

There are very few openings for historians as such – e.g. people specially employed to write official naval or military history, the biography of a famous person or the history of a major company. Such historians and their research assistants are few and far between, but could be employed by organisations such as the Civil Service, British Library, and large specialist museums. You would first need experience in historical research, or archive work or as a writer.

A major source of employment for serious historians is in the educational and academic world. Most of the opportunities are in school teaching, but there are also occasional posts for well-qualified historians to become lecturers and researchers in universities and other institutions of higher education. In this setting, undergraduate and postgraduate lecturing and tutoring is carried out alongside research. Such historians publish their work, which is mainly used by the academic community.

just THE JOB

ARCHAEOLOGIST

> Archaeology is concerned with the remains of the past, which can range from buried towns to minute grains of pollen. Archaeologists research and study information from past societies – their culture and way of life – by examining artefacts, building materials and human and animal remains. There is generally a combination of academic work and field research. Archaeologists have a degree or the equivalent.

Archaeology is a form of detective work, sifting painstakingly through the remains of the past and spending months classifying finds and writing reports. Finding spectacular treasure is rare; a much more common find is a few pot fragments, an animal bone or the remains of a fire. To the true archaeologist, these are as exciting as gold ornaments.

What it takes
Archaeologists need to:

- be keen to understand earlier human society;
- have a wide knowledge of history and a deep knowledge of their specialist period;
- have creative imaginations;
- be painstaking, methodical and thorough;
- show determination combined with great patience;
- be in robust health if they are field archaeologists – necessary for working on digs in all sorts of weather;

- have practical skills in surveying, map-reading and photography;
- understand conservation methods, so that finds can be preserved from rapid deterioration on contact with air;
- understand scientific methods of analysing and dating their finds.

Job opportunities

There is a great interest in our heritage these days, although probably not more than 3000 people are employed as archaeologists in the UK. Although many archaeology graduates do become professional archaeologists, many use the varied skills gained during their degree course to enter a great range of other jobs.

Those who do get jobs as archaeologists work in one of the following areas of employment:

National agencies – *English Heritage* is the principal government agency in charge of ancient monuments. Similar organisations exist in Scotland (*Historic Scotland*) and Wales (*CADW – Welsh Historic Monuments*). English Heritage is an important employer of archaeologists in the roles of inspectors of ancient monuments or historic buildings, or as part of a mobile field team, advising on archaeological activities. Other national bodies such as the *National Trust* and the *National Parks* also employ archaeologists for fieldwork or as education officers, keeping the public informed about sites on their estates. (Addresses are in the Further Information section under Heritage Jobs.)

Museums – this includes the national museums, university museums and smaller collections run by local authorities and societies. The emphasis in museums tends to be on display, administration and a wide range of archaeological topics rather than specialised research and study. Archaeologists are sometimes employed as **education officers**.

Independent units and trusts – most excavation work is carried out by archaeological units, the largest of which employ researchers, archivists, etc, as well as a team of professional excavators. The main purpose of excavation is the recovery of information – the objects which are found at a site and the recording of the features surrounding the find. Archaeological units may be independent trusts or charities; others may be attached to national conservation bodies, museums, local authorities and universities.

Some trusts and research units are financed by central and local government, industry and charitable organisations. These bodies may be concerned with one project (e.g. the *Mary Rose*) or with the archaeology of an area. There are, for example, county archaeological trusts. Their work may include 'rescue archaeology' before a site is developed.

Local authorities – some employ archaeologists on advisory and educational work, and in planning departments. An important part of their job is to keep an inventory of archaeological sites and finds in their area (the SMR – Sites and Monuments record).

Academic work – opportunities for employment in this area are limited, but the work – a combination of research and lecturing – is ideal for the committed archaeologist. Competition for vacancies is strong and preference would be given to applicants with research experience.

Teaching – in further education colleges and schools. To teach archaeology as a specialist subject in schools, you will need to have studied a national curriculum subject alongside archaeology at degree level, and then to have gained a postgraduate teaching qualification. Requirements for teaching in further education are more flexible.

Conservation – specialist work for those with the necessary training. Conservators work mainly in museum laboratories and occasionally in field laboratories on site at a dig. The scientific background for this work is normally acquired through a degree or postgraduate course.

Overseas work – there are opportunities for archaeologists to work on projects overseas. There are British schools of archaeology in Greece, Italy, the Middle East and East Africa. Posts go to experienced researchers and are usually for periods of one to three years.

Advisory work – certain firms of engineers, architects and public utilities employ a number of archaeologists to advise on the impact of development plans on sites of archaeological interest, where they may need to perform investigatory excavations.

TRAINING

Except at the level of willing helper at a dig, with trowel and brush, archaeology is not a school-leaver's job. Almost all archaeologists have a degree, although there are a few opportunities for basic practical work without one. Single-subject courses and ones which combine archaeology with another subject (e.g. history) are widely available.

The minimum requirement for a degree course is two A levels, Advanced GNVQ or a BTEC National Diploma, but an additional A level or equivalent is generally required. Particular A level subjects are not normally specified, and science and humanities subjects are equally valued. Modern languages, especially French and German, are probably more use than Latin or Greek (unless you want to take classical archaeology). Mathematics, physical sciences and languages at GCSE grade C are likely to be useful, and general studies is usually well regarded. Archaeology A level or GCSE is not a requirement, but can be helpful for gaining some idea of what the subject is all about. If you are interested in archaeological conservation, A level sciences, including chemistry, are normally essential.

Although it is an advantage to have taken part in archaeological digs before applying for a degree, it is not essential. In fact, 50% of archaeology students have never been on an excavation. You can take part in short training excavations, details of which are published in *CBA Briefing*.

There are some postgraduate conversion courses for people whose first degree is in a different, but related, subject. For museum work (see later section), a postgraduate vocational qualification is essential.

Mature entrants with suitable qualifications are in general welcomed by archaeology departments, especially if they have good voluntary experience.

National Vocational Qualifications in Environmental Conservation (Archaeology) are available at levels 2, 3 and 4.

Better as a hobby?

As a profession, outside the national agencies, there is little job security and the pay is not particularly good, compared with other graduate employment. However, as a leisure interest, archaeology can easily occupy a lifetime, and much important work is done by volunteers and hobbyists. Volunteers to assist at excavations are always welcome. Under-16s can join the Young Archaeologists' Club (see Further Information section).

ARCHIVIST

> An archivist's main job is the care of written and other records, ancient and modern. Over half of British archivists work in local authorities, with the rest in businesses and other organisations which keep records, such as cathedrals, historic houses and museums. Most archivists are graduates with postgraduate qualifications.

Archivists work with records originating either from institutions or from individuals, which can be used in a variety of ways. Archives may consist of written material, audiotapes and videotapes, films, photographs, and even computer tapes and discs. Archive materials are unique and irreplaceable, and are usually kept in strongrooms to which the public does not have access.

There are many archives throughout the UK, comprising both public and private material. These include:

- **the national archives** – held in the Public Record Office in London, consisting of millions of documents from the Domesday Book onwards;
- **local government records** – records of all the things for which local government bodies are responsible; information inherited from other long-dead authorities, such as workhouse guardians and school boards; collections obtained from private sources;
- **ecclesiastical archives** – great collections in the cathedrals, and registers of baptisms, marriages and burials in parish churches;

- **National Monuments Record** – the public archive of the Royal commission on the Historical Monuments of England: it includes photographs and drawings as well as books and journals.

The types of records which might be preserved include:

- legal and government records;
- records of industrial and commercial organisations and activities;
- ecclesiastical records;
- aristocratic family records;
- records illustrating the social history of people from all walks of life;
- film sequences – documentaries, interviews, news sequences and other broadcast material.

What do archivists do?
- They collect, select and catalogue archives.
- They make their records available to users, and must be able

to guide them to the right documents, so it is important that they are good communicators.
- They use computers to produce catalogues, guides, lists and indexes of their archive material. Preparing lectures, exhibitions and educational material, and helping and advising researchers, are also part of the job.
- They must also destroy records, because, like libraries, many archives are still being added to. Not everything can or should be kept, so archivists must often decide what should be disposed of and what preserved.
- They preserve archives. They must understand the physical properties of materials in their care and provide the necessary conditions for their survival.

TRAINING

Archivists need an academic background, and it helps if they are knowledgeable about social and political history and economics. They need to be able to read handwriting from all periods, to be competent in Latin and to have some knowledge of such things as heraldry and land law. They must be accurate and methodical and, incidentally, be prepared to work in dusty and dirty conditions – not all archives are kept in modern air-conditioned buildings.

It may be possible to start a career as an **archive assistant**, directly after higher education or with A levels or equivalent. Normally, however, archivists start after a one-year postgraduate course in archive administration, recognised by the Society of Archivists. Preferred first degree subjects are history, classics, English, languages or law. Applicants who have done some voluntary vacation work in a local authority record office will have an advantage at selection.

The University of East Anglia offers a one-year MA in Film

Studies which has a film archiving option suitable for those who have completed an undergraduate course in film study.

EMPLOYMENT

More than half of the archivists in Britain work for local government, in museums, record offices or libraries. An increasing number are now working in industry or commerce, where they may be concerned with recent records.

It is not generally very highly paid work, though industrial posts pay better than local or central government ones, or the universities.

HERALDRY & GENEALOGY

> Heraldry and genealogy fascinate a lot of people and are very popular hobbies, particularly genealogy. Unfortunately, there are very few opportunities to work professionally in these fields, and, for most people, they are better kept as leisure interests. However, there are some opportunities for the really determined person.

Genealogy

Genealogists are concerned with searching through the records of the past to find out about the history of families. This means looking through parish registers, census records, letters, wills, deeds of property and court records. In search of these records, genealogists usually work in record offices, but may have to visit churches, local museums, private houses, or perhaps use the services of a local **record-searcher**. Record-searchers or record agents may work part-time or full-time, and perhaps specialise in a certain period, geographical area or subject.

What the work involves

Genealogical research involves historical detective work on documents that may be in bad condition, written in Latin or legal jargon, and perhaps in difficult handwriting. This means that a good education in appropriate subjects is necessary. This could include degree-level study in history, law or archive work. Heraldic knowledge is also useful to genealogists, as coats of arms may often provide clues in a particular line of research. (Genealogists, however, are not able to tell people whether they are entitled to a coat of arms.) When the research is complete, the genealogist will submit a report to the customer, showing how the conclusions have been arrived at. Clients may want information for its own historical sake, or to settle a legal dispute.

Genealogists are sometimes employed to trace the incidence of hereditary diseases and epidemics, assisting medical research.

Heraldry

Heraldry is a more specialised subject than genealogy. The official authority in England, Wales and Northern Ireland is the College of Arms. This has been on the same site in London since 1555, and is a corporation consisting of three Kings of Arms, six Heralds and, below them in rank, four Pursuivants. The College maintains a register of grants of armorial bearings, and registers of pedigrees of armigerous families (those entitled to bear arms) and others. Occasionally, there is a need for an experienced researcher. Heraldic artists and scriveners (or scribes) are employed to paint and write Letters Patent, granting new armorial bearings. They also update and produce new pedigree books, rolls and other calligraphic material. Opportunities are very limited and require considerable flair and imagination. Artists would normally have an art college training, and their work continues the tradition of medieval heraldic illumination in this country.

GETTING STARTED

There are courses in heraldry, genealogy, family history, and palaeography (the study of ancient writing) run by the Centre for Extra-Mural Studies, University of London. Other part-time courses (which do not lead to recognised qualifications) are run by the Society of Genealogists, the Workers Educational Association, university extramural departments, adult education departments in colleges and local/family history societies. These courses can be accredited with qualifications of the Institute of Heraldic and Genealogical Studies.

The Institute offers residential short courses, day schools and a correspondence course, with graded assessments and qualifying examination. The Institute's certificate and diploma are widely recognised qualifications in the profession. There is a scheme which involves paying for your training by undertaking research for the Institute's business organisation.

Books on researching family history are widely available in libraries and bookshops, and would certainly help to get you started. You should also find useful material on heraldry and other related areas.

EMPLOYMENT PROSPECTS

The prospects of a well-paid career in heraldry and genealogy are not good, and most training courses are undertaken at your own expense. So it might be better to get qualifications and first employment in some related career, such as working in archives, librarianship or perhaps history teaching. You could then pursue your interest as a hobby at first, and your qualifications and experience might eventually lead to professional work. You might even start up a small part-time practice, specialising in particular types of records as a record agent. The Association of Genealogists and Record Agents is a professional body, membership of which is intended to indicate high standards of work.

Lecturing is one possible area of employment, and there are occasional opportunities in the field of heraldic and genealogical journalism, in specialist and local history magazines. *Debrett's Peerage* is directly concerned with genealogical matters, and has to be revised periodically. However, as with other aspects of work in this field, full-time employment is very unlikely.

just THE JOB

HERITAGE JOBS

> Heritage work covers those careers and jobs which are concerned with the historical buildings and sites found everywhere around the British Isles. It includes management, maintenance and restoration of sites, as well as their development from a leisure and tourism point of view. As you can imagine, this means there are jobs for people with a wide range of qualifications.

Heritage sites are not just castles and stately homes. Increasingly, things like historic industrial sites and transport systems are being seen as valuable elements of our history, and worthy of being preserved and restored.

There is a great mixture of employers in this kind of work. The organisation which has taken over the running of the nationally owned sites in England is *English Heritage*. Many of the most famous historic sites – like Stonehenge and Dover Castle – are run by English Heritage, or, to give it its official title, the Historic Buildings and Monuments Commission for England. They have responsibility for many other sites of historic or archaeological interest, such as iron age villages, ruined monasteries, etc. There are separate government bodies in Northern Ireland (*Northern Ireland Environment and Heritage Service*), Wales (*CADW – Welsh Historic Monuments*) and Scotland (*Historic Scotland*) responsible for heritage sites in those countries.

The other major organisation is the *National Trust*, with its wonderful collection of historic houses, parks and unspoiled countryside and coastline.

A considerable number of other historic sites and buildings are owned by local authorities or by trusts and charities and, of course, there are many historic houses that are still the homes of their owners. Also, one should not forget the Church of England, with its magnificent cathedrals, some of the most popular places for tourists and visitors. Westminster Abbey, for example, is so popular that visitors have to queue up to get in at peak times.

The variety of all these sites is enormous and the choice and type of employment opportunities is equally great. Think of the problems of running and preserving somewhere like Dover Castle, with its many visitors each day throughout the year, needing to be entertained, informed, directed and refreshed. Contrast that with the work of a trust restoring a canal for navigation, rebuilding locks, clearing rubbish and mud from the waterway, and making decisions about fishing and boating.

What jobs are there?

With this range of potential employers, it is very difficult to generalise about job opportunities and the kinds of people required. English Heritage is a major employer, with jobs for architects, archaeologists and surveyors as well as administrative jobs. However, the competition for what jobs there are is fierce, and staff are more frequently recruited as administrative assistants, or as administrative officers – a post requiring five GCSEs at grade C, including English language, or equivalent.

The National Trust is also a relatively large employer, but tends to favour applicants with experience (and also, incidentally, encourages applications from people with special needs). The National Trust produces a fortnightly vacancy bulletin.

Professional-level jobs are usually advertised in the national press. Service jobs at heritage sites and buildings are advertised locally, as are jobs at sites owned by local authorities.

Several heritage conservationists work with environmental pressure groups.

The main kinds of employment and training are:

Preserving and restoring

Time, weather and nature are the great enemies of historic buildings and sites. The great cathedrals have teams of craftworkers constantly restoring the ravages of frost, wind, acid rain and deathwatch beetle, as well as undertaking major works like restoring Salisbury's spire, the western face of Wells Cathedral or York's transept. Many historic buildings were built to last, but five or six hundred years may be asking rather a lot. Stonemasons, carpenters, roof tilers and plumbers are never likely to run short of work on our historic buildings – as long as there's somebody to foot the bill.

It is not only the structure of ancient buildings that needs preservation. Many of them are treasure houses of paintings, sculpture, tapestries, carpets, musical instruments and furniture. A constant programme of repair, cleaning and renewal is essential, so that these treasures can be passed on to succeeding generations. Expert knowledge is vital in this work to avoid irreparable damage. You cannot take a seventeenth-century silk-thread tapestry down to the dry cleaners! Many objects need to be kept in a particular kind of atmosphere: too much dryness can be as great a problem as too much damp.

GETTING STARTED

To get into this sort of work, you could consider various routes. Many of the major heritage sites have workshops where apprentices can learn the skills of maintaining and restoring ancient buildings. Basic building-trade skills like bricklaying and carpentry can also be adapted to old techniques, so training in the construction industry could be relevant. There are BA degree courses in Heritage Studies and BSc degree courses in Heritage Conservation, Building Conservation Technology and Environmental Protection. There are other relevant degree courses: look in the higher education handbooks under conservation.

Both apprenticeship training and college training have their advantages/disadvantages when considering a suitable career path. A good route could be to serve an apprenticeship as a trainee mason (or carpenter or glazier), for instance in a cathedral workshop. The restoration of fabrics and paintings involves specialised skills which can be learned on full-time and part-time courses. (See later section on art restoration.)

Recording and researching

Historical understanding of ancient sites and buildings does not stand still. Archaeologists and historians continue to discover new things about even the best-known sites. The better we understand sites, the better equipped we are to preserve and restore them, and to help visitors to understand them. In the main, historians and archaeologists are academics based in universities, though there are also opportunities with English Heritage and, very occasionally, with local authorities which have a major heritage site in their charge.

As well as research, there is also archive and library work to be done. One of the largest employers in this field is the Royal Commission on the Historical Monuments of England which, together with the National Monuments Record, is based at Swindon in Wiltshire. All the cathedrals have libraries with collections of ancient manuscripts of great value and interest. Many of the large stately homes have libraries and collections of historic documents and records. Archivists and librarians are needed to record, catalogue and preserve all these records of the past, so that they are available to modern researchers for the foreseeable future.

Administration

At any heritage site, there are all sorts of interests that have to be combined and balanced. There are the needs of visitors and tourists, of historians and archaeologists, landowners and farmers.

Managers must ensure that:

- a site is accessible in the present, but preserved for the future;
- funds are raised for conservation and development;
- the day-to-day running is carefully organised;
- staff are recruited, trained and supervised;
- car parks, toilets and ordering catering supplies are attended to.

Running a site that is a major tourist attraction can be like operating a museum, a shop and a restaurant, all at the same time. Managers of historic properties are often asked to give talks to meetings about their site.

With this variety of work to be done, the backgrounds of people employed as warden/administrators or estate managers are equally varied. Any experience in retail, hotel and catering, leisure and recreation or financial management is likely to be of use. Although work with tourists is concentrated in the summer months, the winter season involves working with maintenance contractors.

There are also opportunities in surveying or conservation where organisations hold large properties or big areas of land – for instance, the National Trust. The University of Birmingham, in conjunction with the Ironbridge Gorge Museum, runs a postgraduate course in Industrial Heritage.

Tourism, marketing and publicity

A major concern for the management of a heritage attraction is getting visitors to come, and ensuring that they enjoy their visit when they get there. There may be a need for guides at the site (though in the case of the National Trust and most cathedrals, these guides are voluntary workers).

Leaflets, guidebooks, maps, charts and diagrams have to be designed, commissioned and printed. There may also be publicity material to produce and put in the right place to attract visitors. Special publicity may be needed for exhibitions, battle re-enactments or concert series, in drives to raise funds for restoration work. Often, school parties or historical societies

want to visit, and special arrangements may have to be made. There is often a need for liaison with local and regional tourist boards, to ensure that the site is publicised in their publications and that details of particular attractions, times of opening and entry charges are all correct.

To get into this kind of work at management level requires training and experience in such areas as travel and tourism, marketing or public relations. Within tourism and marketing, an interest in a particular site and the ability to use a wordprocessor may get you a basic job, which could eventually lead to higher things.

Service jobs

Any large heritage attraction needs staff to do all sorts of basic jobs serving the public. There are jobs in catering, cleaning, car park attending, gardening and working in the shops that so many sites now have. Most of these jobs are seasonal and/or part-time, as the major influx of visitors is in the summer. Many places are completely closed to the public from November to the end of March, but caretakers are required all year round, often on a residential basis.

Education/information officer

One way of making a visit to a heritage site attractive is to help people to understand what they are seeing. Major heritage sites are increasingly concerned with educating visitors who come to the site, and going out to schools to interest the young in the history and background of the site.

People appointed as education/information officers are likely to have had teaching experience. They need to be the sort of person who can communicate well with groups of mainly young people. It also helps to be interested in writing and researching material, and getting involved in the production of leaflets, workbooks and visual displays, including slides and videos.

MUSEUM WORK

> Museums gather together different kinds of objects, artefacts and associated materials, classify them, preserve, exhibit and store them for the benefit of the general public. There are between 2000 and 2500 museums and galleries in Britain, employing about 40,000 people. These include not only local authority museums, but also the many independent museums, both regional and national. There are opportunities for those with qualifications ranging from good GCSEs, or their equivalent, to degree level and beyond.

What the work involves

Museum work could be for you if you:

- are interested in objects and their environment;
- like building up collections;
- enjoy describing and documenting articles;
- care about restoring and preserving artefacts;
- are good at display;
- can make their collections appealing to young and old alike;
- like working with the public;
- can communicate your enthusiasm to the public.

Not all glass cases

Museums today have usually shed their image of being dull, silent places. Now, their collections are displayed in imaginative and lively ways to bring the past alive to visitors. Museum visiting is a very popular leisure activity, attracting over 110 million people a year. The days when everything was in glass cases have long gone and collections have accessible 'interactive' displays to make topics meaningful to adults and children alike. If you have visited major museums like the Natural History Museum or the Science Museum in London, you will know what exciting exhibitions are mounted. You will also find that many of the smaller museums now take an educational approach to their displays. Many try to actively involve their visitors – for instance Blists Hill Open Air Museum at Ironbridge and the Beamish Open Air Museum in County Durham.

SPECIALISATION

In museum work, you can specialise according to your skills and interests. There are jobs which are mainly administrative or educational, and others where you work very closely with objects to conserve and restore them. The work also varies according to the type of collection – some museums specialise in just one type of collection, others house general collections or combine several specialisms.

There are small museums and departments of large museums which specialise in areas such as fine arts, decorative arts, archaeology and industrial archaeology, folk life and local history, natural history, science, technology, costumes and textiles, militaria, toys, vehicles, photography, marine subjects, and many more.

It is difficult to generalise about the types of work done by museum staff, as often the things which make an individual job interesting are the 'one-off' duties.

Curator

Curators are responsible for the organisation of a museum, or for a department of a large museum. Sometimes they have responsibility for a number of collections on different sites, such as all the museums and galleries belonging to the local council in one town. In other cases, the curator may be in charge of a small museum and must perform a whole range of different tasks.

What it takes
Curators need to be able to:

- acquire objects for the museum;
- identify and catalogue them;
- label and display them to the best advantage;
- inform and educate the public through audio-visual presentations, lectures, leaflets and other back-up material relating to exhibits;
- publicise the museum;
- deal with enquiries from the public or academics;
- give talks at local clubs, women's groups, etc, and perhaps run a junior museum club;
- manage the other museum staff.

Museum curators are expected to be scholars. But, as well as having the necessary academic background to care for and develop a collection, they have to be equally good at staff management, general and financial administration and organisation, especially in small museums. In effect, they have to run a small business.

In very large museums, there is more scope for some staff (**research officers**) to concentrate on academic research work, while others take care of the administrative side. Those wishing to concentrate on management can study part-time for qualifications in administration and management. Postgraduate courses in museum management are offered at the City, Newcastle, Hull and Edinburgh universities.

Curators normally have a lot of say in the way their museum or department is organised and how their budget is allocated. This level of work is achieved only after experience. Whilst the curator takes overall responsibility, **assistant curators** cope with the daily running of the museum. They might typically spend half their time on administrative work, and the rest on public enquiries and researching new publications and display materials.

ENTRY AND QUALIFICATIONS

Assistant curator is the level of job at which you could expect to start as a graduate entrant. There are also, in the larger museums, some jobs for **museum assistants** with good GCSEs, or qualifications of A level standard, to help with the more routine work. But, usually, to enter curatorial work, an honours degree in one or more of the following subjects is needed (according to the type of collection): anthropology, archaeology, history, art history, classics, science, technology. Art galleries prefer a degree in art, art history or art and design.

These days, it is also advantageous to have a higher degree – preferably, a specialist museum qualification. Graduate trainees usually learn on-the-job, sometimes through formal graduate training programmes. There are also full-time and part-time vocational courses for graduates in art gallery and/or museum studies. The Museum Training Institute publishes a list of courses with a museums element.

Adults: note that maturity and previous experience may mean that stated entry requirements can be relaxed.

Avril – assistant curator in a town museum

'I spent three years at university, gaining a degree in history. I wanted to work in a museum, as I had done some voluntary work in my local museum during the holidays and loved it.

The work is so varied. I am currently carrying out research on some kitchen equipment that has been donated to the museum. I have to find out what the pieces were used for, how old they are, and then record them on the computer. We are also putting on an exhibition next month, showing what life was like in this town during the first and second world wars. My job is to gather in old photos, and try to work out who the people were, where they were and what they were doing. As we're not a large museum, I have to take my turn at writing the exhibition labels, dealing with public enquiries and doing some routine administration, but I don't mind as it is giving me a wide experience, which will help me get promotion.

My dream is to work in the National History Museum, but in order to get anywhere near achieving that, I need much more experience. I'll probably have to spend a few years moving around the country, working in different museums.'

Conservation staff

Conservation staff examine objects and paintings to see what needs to be done in the way of cleaning and repair. Technical, scientific and practical skills are important, and staff develop their abilities to the full only after considerable experience. Generally, staff specialise in particular types of restoration. Some

work concerns archaeological materials, but experts are also needed for work on pictures (perhaps for particular periods of painting), sculpture, textiles, and so on.

Besides special skills in handling materials, good colour vision and lots of patience, it is necessary to know about the history and the technology of the period to which objects in the collection belong. Some museums have laboratories and employ scientists and technologists to work as a team with conservators. Most conservation posts are with larger museums, although there are some in the smaller museums, and similar work is carried out in connection with the antiques trade. Conservation includes controlling the museum environment so that exhibits do not deteriorate.

ENTRY REQUIREMENTS

A level science (especially chemistry)/Advanced GNVQ/BTEC qualifications or a degree in a science provide a very useful background, and graduates are increasingly preferred. There are also specialist courses dealing with particular types of conservation.

Design staff, modelmakers, taxidermists, photographers, etc

These specialists are employed by bigger museums, but not in large numbers. In small museums, one person often needs multiple skills. Larger museums may have a department for the preparation of exhibitions, and also a design department.

Relevant specialisms are:
- three-dimensional design for planning and constructing temporary and permanent exhibitions;
- graphic design for exhibitions, catalogues, posters, labelling of the collection, design and layout of publications, etc;
- modelmaking for all types of collections, including natural history, science, technology, archaeology, marine collections, etc;
- taxidermy for natural history collections;
- photography for display and exhibition work, etc, and also recording specimens, including site work on excavations, etc.

ENTRY REQUIREMENTS

For design staff and photographers, an appropriate professional training is generally needed. The University of Lincolnshire and Humberside offers a BA Honours degree in museum and exhibition design, and a BTEC HND in exhibition and heritage display is offered at Mid-Warwickshire College. There are BTEC HND courses in exhibition design at Berkshire College of Art & Technology, Bournemouth and Poole College of Art & Design, Central College of Commerce, the University of Lincolnshire and Humberside, and Dewsbury College. BTEC HND courses in modelmaking are available from South Devon College, Suffolk College and the Kent Institute of Art and Design. For course listings and details, consult the ECCTIS database or the Laser *Compendium of Higher Education* in your local career centres. For detailed information on training, consult the CRAC *Directory of Higher Education*.

Educational staff

Museum educational staff help visitors of all ages to learn from museum collections. They may prepare publications and information packs, give talks, etc, and sometimes organise loan services to schools and colleges. General publicity and public relations may also be part of the job, as well as writing and design. There may be other duties such as organising and running junior museum clubs, talking to local clubs as a guest speaker, and so on. It is usually necessary to have teaching qualifications and experience, preferably with a degree, or a strong interest, in a subject relevant to the museum's collection. The London Institute of Education offers an MA course entitled 'Museums and Galleries in Education'. For further information on educational work in museums, contact the Museum Studies Department at Leicester University (see Further Information section).

TRAINING

The Museum Training Institute (MTI) now provides a training and qualifications structure for all areas of museum, gallery and heritage work. National Vocational Qualifications are available up to and including level 5.

FINDING A VACANCY OR TRAINING PLACE

Jobs and training courses in museum work are extremely popular and competitive, so get the best qualifications you can before you apply. Determination and enthusiasm are essential. Visit as many museums and galleries as you can. Be able to talk knowledgeably about a special interest, and try to add some experience to your academic qualifications – get involved on a voluntary basis with archaeological digs, the local museum, a conservation project, etc.

Vacancies are advertised in the quality national press and specialist journals, including the *Museums Journal* available from the Museums Association. Some posts at lower levels (e.g. for technicians and assistants) may be advertised locally only, and some posts in national museums are recruited through the Civil Service.

CAREERS IN ART GALLERIES

> Running a successful public art gallery requires a great deal of activity behind the scenes. A lot of work goes into mounting a varied programme of exhibitions to entice a large viewing public. All the jobs involved need an appreciation of art. There are opportunities ranging from those requiring a few GCSEs, or their equivalent, to work requiring degree- and postgraduate-level qualifications.

Works of art are displayed in public art galleries. Galleries can vary greatly, not only in size and number, but also in the range of creative pieces on display.

- Large galleries, such as the National Gallery of London or the National Gallery of Scotland, hold important and valuable collections of paintings and sculptures.
- Provincial museums may have rooms set aside as galleries for art works.
- Galleries funded by local authorities sometimes house collections with a special theme, such as the work of a particular artist, or artists, from the region.
- There are many displays of collected art works throughout the country, which may be owned by university departments, colleges, hospitals or private individuals.

In commercial art galleries, it is important to draw up displays of paintings, textiles and sculptures which interest both new purchasers and regular collectors. They are mostly situated in the cities, which attract tourists. Visitors can purchase 'old masters', or modern paintings by local artists which depict scenes portraying the lifestyle of the local area. In some cities, a number of such galleries are gathered together, as in London's Bond Street or the Left Bank area of Paris. Serious collectors may call regularly to discover the works of established painters and sculptors which have entered the market, or to select examples from new and talented artists. Small galleries often specialise in the works of a school of artists or in paintings from particular periods, such as early portraits, 18th-century landscapes in oils, 19th-century water colours. Remember that, in private galleries, the purpose is to *sell* rather than simply to exhibit, and the pay is usually set at a low basic rate enhanced by commission earned on sales!

What the work involves

There is a variety of work involved in running a gallery, whether it is a national gallery open to the public, a small public collection in a town, or a commercial gallery.

Building up a public collection

Depending upon the size of the establishment, one or several people have to take responsibility for maintaining and consolidating the gallery's collection of art works. Money from grants, donations, entrance fees and the like is used for the purchase of important items. These art works may be needed to complete a collection, or because they are examples of new work.

Conserving the art works

In public galleries, the collection has to be regularly checked so that any necessary cleaning or conservation work can be prescribed and carried out. In the larger galleries, conservation work is performed by in-house conservators, while smaller galleries often employ freelance experts. Conditions under which art works are stored, displayed and transported need to be monitored, as light levels, humidity and vibration can all cause damage.

Exhibition organising
Exhibitions have to be arranged in a manner that shows an understanding of the art works themselves, and of the expectations and needs of the viewers. It is essential to have some knowledge of art and art history to do this job well. Careful layout is necessary with some modern pieces, where the organiser has to consider the intentions of the artist.

Promotional work
Each event mounted by the gallery may require special fundraising and promotion, with the preparation of photographs and information to make posters, brochures and catalogues for the public. This work has to be done accurately and usually to a tight deadline. Visiting lecturers may be asked to give talks about the particular artists and their works.

Educational work
Some local authority galleries employ a qualified teacher to construct an educational programme aimed at helping local schoolchildren to analyse and enjoy paintings. This work can develop into practical drawing sessions, illustrated talks and visits to other major galleries. The Institute of Education in London offers a postgraduate MA course entitled 'Museums and Galleries in Education'.

Security work
Security is a high priority in an art gallery and, where larger collections are open to the public, many people are employed as gallery attendants – inspecting bags, watching the behaviour of individuals, and generally making sure that the art works entrusted to their keeping are safe.

Art loans work
Those art galleries which sell new works often operate a hire system whereby members of the public, businesses or institutions can have a changing display for little expenditure. The cost

of the loan can become part of an eventual purchase and it has been found that, through a lending system, people often become sufficiently fond of a work to buy it outright. This borrowing system has to be carefully administered.

What it takes

Although every art gallery is unique, there are common areas of work for which a basic understanding of art is important. Many people employed in positions of responsibility in galleries have a degree in fine art, the history of art, or art and design, but for specialised work you need to able to offer a postgraduate diploma (for instance, in art history or conservation techniques) or give evidence of similar, specialist training.

There are many administrative tasks to be completed in the largest galleries, for which secretaries and administrative assistants are employed. An artistic background is not necessary for these posts, nor for the security posts. If you were looking for a position as a curator in an art gallery, you would need an art training, but you should be prepared to work long, irregular hours for a fairly small remuneration.

In small public galleries, the directors cover most of the work themselves, with the assistance of one curator and possibly a secretary. These assistants may be part-time or even voluntary workers who have a real interest in the works of art, or in promoting creativity amongst local artists. Part-time assistants are sometimes needed when exhibitions are mounted.

In private and commercial galleries, there has to be a high level of communication and involvement with the public to whom you hope to sell a work of art. With modern works, it would be essential to have gathered background knowledge about the different artists.

TRAINING

A significant number of people working in art galleries have gained a degree or HND in some aspects of art or art history. The vast majority of art and design courses are applied for through UCAS. There is tremendous competition for most fine art degree courses and, as such, it is only a minority of places that go to applicants straight from school. The majority of successful applicants have first completed a college-based preparatory course (e.g. a one-year Art Foundation, BTEC National Diploma, adult Access or GNVQ Advanced). A number of institutions offer postgraduate courses in gallery studies.

EMPLOYMENT

Vacancies for jobs in art galleries are listed in the *Museums Journal*, published monthly by the Museum Association; *Leisure News*, the bi-monthly journal of AIM (the Association of Independent Museums); the *Guardian*, in the creative and media section on Mondays and the education section on Tuesdays; *The Times* and its supplements, the *Independent* and *Time Out*. Local newspapers are used to advertise junior posts.

Sotheby's auction house runs its own diploma courses and also has a follow-up careers service for attending students, which offers lectures on career topics, and an unofficial placement system.

Overall, job prospects are not high, as the total number of staff working in art galleries is very small. It helps if you have gained some experience of working in galleries, perhaps on a voluntary basis.

University galleries are run by members of the teaching academic staff, with administrative assistance.

WORKING IN ANTIQUES

> The antiques business is concerned with selling, buying and valuation. It gives you the chance to work with old and often beautiful things, but it is still very much a business, where making a profit is essential. Interest and enthusiasm can be more important than academic qualifications.

While antiques are technically objects over 100 years old, almost anything can be collectable: books, furniture, jewellery, clothing, china, toys and domestic utensils. Objects from the quite recent past are often described as bric-a-brac rather than antiques. Although it helps to enjoy old and beautiful objects, a shrewd business sense and an eye for a bargain are essential. It is also a business where getting on easily with people is important. Customers, after all, don't *have* to buy antiques and it is often subtle selling techniques which clinch a deal.

GETTING STARTED

As has already been suggested, the range of objects loosely described as antiques is very wide. At one end is the market stall heaped with interesting junk collected from jumble sales; at the other, the auctioneer from Sotheby's knocking down a Rubens for five million pounds. The range of qualifications and background required can be equally varied. Top auction houses often prefer someone with an art history degree; your local junk shop may just be looking for a pair of strong arms to heave old sofas around and, probably, a driving licence!

The essential thing is to gain experience, to actually handle antiques. Go to museums and stately homes, attend auctions and make contacts. You will also find a wide range of books from which to learn about antiques and their collection. Apart from the grand end of the market, most businesses are small (over

20,000 of them) and there is little formal training. The best way to start is to go round antique shops asking for a job. A local auction room might be another possibility, perhaps as a porter fetching and carrying at auctions. Here you would become familiar with the names of items, their construction and also the price that they currently fetch at auction. Helping at a weekend market might be another way of getting experience – even running your own junk stall, if you are confident and yet prepared to make mistakes!

EDUCATION AND TRAINING

There is relatively little formal training, and much of that is privately run and expensive. If you are capable of work to degree standard, you might consider art history as a suitable course. This will give you a knowledge of painting and sculpture and the upper end of the antiques market (e.g. oriental prints, Middle Eastern carpets and so forth) but perhaps less knowledge of Georgian or Victorian furniture, arts, crafts, vases, textiles, etc – the less grand side of the business.

For art history degrees, you normally need three A levels (or the equivalent) including one, and preferably two, languages from French, German, Latin and Italian. Southampton Institute of Higher Education offers a BA honours and MA degree courses in Fine Art Evaluation, which give exemption from ISVA (Incorporated Society of Valuers and Auctioneers) exams. You can also study for ISVA qualifications part-time or by home-study if in a relevant job.

Farnborough College of Technology offers a two-year, full-time HND in Antiques and Collection Management.

Private courses
Some private courses are intended for future professionals; others are more for the interested amateur. These courses are

not cheap and they cannot guarantee you a job, but they can be very helpful (NB local authority grants are unlikely to be available). You may also find evening classes in your area, though these are essentially aimed at the interested amateur. The following are a few of the better-known course providers:

Christie's Education – 63 Old Brompton Road, London SW7 3JS.
The Courtauld Institute of Art – Somerset House, Strand, London WC2R 0RN.
Inchbald School of Design – 7 Eaton Gate, London SW1W 9BA.
Sotheby's Institute – 30 Oxford Street, London W1R 1RE.
Study Centre for the History of the Fine and Decorative Arts – 21 Palace Gardens Terrace, London W8 4SA.
The Victoria and Albert Museum – Cromwell Road, London SW7 2RL.

Repair and restoration courses
The next section looks at the restoration and conservation of works of art, which is really a quite separate area of work. There are various courses in restoring ordinary antiques, both full- and part-time. In many areas of antique restoration it may be possible to be apprenticed to a skilled restorer rather than going to college.

West Dean College – West Dean, Chichester PO18 0QZ. Tel: 01243 811301
This is a college for arts and crafts, specialising in the restoration of antiques. Courses are offered in the conservation and restoration of clocks, fine metalwork restoration, furniture, musical instruments, porcelain and ceramics, rare books and manuscripts.

The following are just some examples of other courses available:

Embroidery and fabrics
Royal School of Needlework – Hampton Court Palace, East Molesey KT8 9AU.
The Textile Conservation Centre – same address.

Clocks
British Horological Institute – Upton Hall, Upton, Newark NG23 5TE.
Hackney Community College – Keltan House, 89–115 Mare Street, London E8 4RG.

Furniture
Buckinghamshire College of Brunel University – Queen Alexandra Road, High Wycombe, Buckinghamshire HP11 2JZ.
London Guildhall University – 41 Commercial Road, London E1 1LA.
Manchester College of Arts and Technology – Lower Hardman Street, Manchester M3 3ER.
Rural Development Commission – 141 Castle Street, Salisbury.
Ryecotewood College – Priest End, Thame, Oxfordshire OX9 2AF.

Musical Instruments
London Guildhall University – 41 Commercial Road, London E1 1LA.
Newark and Sherwood College – Friary Road, Newark, NG24 1BP.

Pictures
Royal College of Art (in conjunction with the Victoria and Albert Museum and Imperial College of Science, Technology and Medicine) – Kensington Gore, London SW7 2EU.

just THE JOB

RESTORING WORKS OF ART

> Restoration and conservation is a very complex and painstaking business, but it can be extremely rewarding work. It's about giving a new lease of life to objects which have deteriorated over the years. The training is long and involves learning about the scientific side of the work, as well as art history and practical skills.

Restoration work may be on a very large scale, such as the restoration of works of art which were badly damaged after the fire at Hampton Court Palace. Or, it may be restoring carpets for the National Trust. Whatever the task, the work involves something unique, delicate and valuable (if not priceless). Everything that is collectable may need conserving at some stage. Today, conservation work is not only found in the traditional fields of fine art, archaeology, furniture and ceramics, but also with glassware, sculpture, musical instruments and books.

Restorer

All works of art suffer from the passage of time. Acid rain corrodes statues; the varnish on paintings turns brown with age and misuse. In some cases the artists have used a medium which has deteriorated with the course of time. They may have used a pigment which was not chemically stable and the colours in a painting have totally altered. Even the base material on which a work was done does not last for ever. In the past, works of art have been altered by other hands, figures added or painted out. There is also the question of whether you **restore** a work to what it may have been, or **conserve** it, preserving it as it is at present for future generations.

Obviously, the background knowledge, skills and understanding necessary to make these kinds of decisions are not things you can acquire overnight. Add to that a working knowledge of materials and their behaviour, the necessary technical skills, and the sheer stamina required to spend hundreds of hours on one job, and you will begin to get some feeling for the nature of the work. Imagine the hours of painstaking work involved in removing a painting from the decaying canvas on which it was painted, and relaying it on a new backcloth. On a larger scale, consider the ten-plus years it took to restore the sculpture and stonework on the spire of Salisbury Cathedral.

Tony – antique furniture restorer

'There is a very satisfying element to work which breathes life into a formerly beautiful object, whether it is a footstool, a hand-carved four poster bed or a rocking chair for a wet nurse. To bring about the change from a dusty, broken, misused and discarded object into a useful and highly attractive piece of usable furniture is immensely gratifying. Although the furniture doesn't belong to me, (all too highly priced, once it has passed through my hands!), I do have the satisfaction of listening to admiring comment and the knowledge that the particular antique piece will be admired by a least two more generations, because of my efforts.

I had no intention of doing restoration work after leaving college. I had taken a degree in English, and worked for several years in a popular bookshop before even looking at an antique. During the winter months, I collected driftwood washed up on the nearby beach and made some very individual sculptures and tables from the larger trunks. This interest had developed into woodcarving. I found myself examining the objects in antique shop windows and studying books on antique furniture to discover old motifs of plant forms that took my fancy, and which were not too difficult for me to copy or adapt in my carvings.

Eventually, I spent so much time examining old pieces in a second-hand and antique warehouse, that they recognised my interest and offered me money to restore some carved chairs which needed new frieze-work. That was it. I enjoyed the job so much that, although the pay was low initially, I agreed to work for the firm full-time, leaving the bookshop.

I have never looked back! There is something new to learn in this work every day. I have done my own research, and discovered for myself how to make a french polish the exact colour of 16th-century oak or 18th-century walnut, but young people could save a lot of time by doing a restoration course first, or alongside their job. Many tricks of the trade are best passed down from older craftsmen in the field. My knowledge has all had to be garnered at first hand.

Now I am in my tenth year here. I have gradually tackled harder jobs as my experience has broadened, and I do outside work for several other antique businesses which are too small to employ a full-time restorer. There is plenty of freelance work for a responsible self-employed worker in this field. My income has grown and, who knows, I may yet own my own antique business outright and give advice to my own trainees on restoration!

Conservator

To be a conservator you need to:

- be interested in all sorts of objects, and their history;
- know how they were produced;
- have some scientific knowledge;
- be patient and painstaking;
- have good eyesight and colour vision.

Where conservators and restorers work
The public sector
This includes the famous national museums and galleries, like the British Museum and the National Gallery, and many other

galleries all round the country which are run by local authorities, universities and trusts. There is also work with English Heritage and the equivalent Scottish and Welsh bodies.

The private sector

There has been quite an expansion in the numbers of firms in this sector. In the main, private firms are very small businesses which specialise in a particular area of work. They contract to carry out restoration and conservation work for private collectors, antique dealers, auctioneers, owners of historic houses and the National Trust. Private sector conservators may have started direct from a college course, or learned their trade in public sector organisations, or through an apprenticeship to a specialist.

DEVELOPING YOUR CAREER

There is a limited career structure in the public sector, but moving up in an organisation usually means moving away from practical work to more managerial work. In the private sector, your prospects depend very much on the success of the business, which will mean having business skills as well as being a good restorer.

TRAINING

There is a wide range of courses at art colleges, further and higher education colleges, universities and private colleges. Painting and archaeological restoration/conservation are usually offered as postgraduate courses. For these postgraduate courses you will need a first degree in art history or science. Other areas, such as furniture, textiles, ceramics and books and manuscripts, are offered at various entry levels. In addition, it may be possible to be apprenticed to a restorer, particularly in such specialisations as textiles, furniture and stone-carving.

WORKING IN LIBRARIES & INFORMATION SERVICES

> Library and information work involves working with books, computer databases and with all the other modern methods of storing information. There is work for highly qualified professionals and more routine work for library assistants, all of whom can now work towards nationally recognised NVQs in information and library service work.

Library and information work is a career about which people think they know quite a lot. There's the TV stereotype character – bespectacled, fumbling and shy, working in a dull, dusty place. But it's hardly a typical or accurate picture of modern librarians or information officers and their places of work!

Some misconceptions

There are perhaps four main misunderstandings about working in libraries and information services.

'Librarians are people who check your books in and out of the library, and put all the returned books back on the shelves.'
In fact, two main types of staff work in libraries – chartered librarians and information professionals, and library assistants. These are quite different jobs (though in very small libraries there is more overlap). Library assistants normally see to the routine running of the library. Librarians and information

specialists are highly qualified professionals whose duties are described below.

'Librarians and assistants spend all of their time with books.'
This is no longer the case. Books are just one means of storing information so that it can be found again. In public libraries, cassettes, CDs, and videos are all part of the library stock. Increasingly, systems other than print are used for storing information. Computers and viewdata systems are used very frequently to find information. Pages of print can be microfilmed to be viewed through an enlarger when required. These applications of new technology mean that information can be stored much more economically and found much more rapidly and efficiently; it is possible to access information on computers all over the world!

'Library and information work is a good career for someone who doesn't like mixing with other people.'
Not true at all! To be a good provider of information, you have to get on with people, understand their requirements and be able to communicate clearly. You also have to cope with grumblers and people who cannot articulate their enquiries very well.

'Most librarians work in public libraries.'
These are the only libraries and information services that many people know about, apart from school and college libraries and resource centres. But in fact, whereas not long ago at least half of all librarians worked in public libraries, they now account for only 28% of members of the Library Association. There is increasing employment for librarians in other sectors of business and industry, news broadcasting and journalism, wherever there are information needs.

Where library and information professionals work

Besides public lending libraries, the other main types of libraries are:

- public reference libraries and information services – often a department of the public library (as is the lending library), but may be housed in a separate library building;
- academic libraries in universities, colleges, etc;
- the national libraries;
- special libraries and information services for industry, commerce, government departments, medicine, the law, etc;
- libraries in schools;
- careers centre libraries;
- libraries in hospitals, prisons, etc.

Academic libraries in universities, colleges, and research institutes contain many specialist academic books, periodicals, documents and databases. Each subject division is usually staffed by specialists. An academic librarian is very involved with the resourcing of courses, authorising loans from other libraries and assisting students in finding the information they need.

The national libraries include the British Library, the National Library of Scotland, the National Library of Wales and the National Art Library. They are huge libraries of great importance, with many specialist subject staff who provide a service to those seeking very diverse information.

Specialist libraries and information services, which serve particular groups of users, include the House of Commons library, BBC libraries, newspapers, government departments, scientific research organisations, architectural and legal practices, etc. Big companies have financial libraries, major hospitals have medical libraries, and industries have libraries containing all the specialist information on the technologies, raw materials and processes which they use. Special libraries may hold textual, musical and pictorial materials in the form of pamphlets, periodicals, research reports, musical scores, microfilms, videodiscs, compact discs and subscribe to on-line databases, etc.

The collections may be small, with the librarian or information officer also spending some time working as a researcher.

School and college libraries are found in technical, agricultural, music and art colleges. Schools may just offer library assistant or clerical assistant posts, but, in most areas, secondary school and college libraries are managed by fully qualified professional staff.

What do library and information professionals do?

The work of librarians (or information officers) and their assistants varies a lot, according to where they are employed.

They **select** books, periodicals, magazines, cassettes and other materials. They must carefully balance the needs of their users against the available resources. In a public or general interest library, an awareness of local tastes, authors, subjects and publishers is essential to achieve greatest effect. In the public library service, library and information staff often choose books and other materials as a team, sharing their knowledge. In a special or academic library, the users may influence decisions on which items are to be bought.

They **research** information to help users solve a particular problem. The librarian or information officer uses reference books, bibliographies, periodicals and magazines, computer databases or any other available source to provide the best possible answer to the person making the enquiry. This detective work can be a great source of job satisfaction, and forms a high proportion of the work in all types of libraries. In a public library, the enquiries can be very wide-ranging: helping children with homework topics, adults undertaking independent learning or doing quizzes and competitions or wanting information on foreign countries, local authors researching historical information, etc. In academic and special libraries, complex enquiries are likely to need a good knowledge of the subject and bring the librarian into contact with other special information collections, using all kinds of new technology.

The librarian or information officer in an academic or a special library may be involved in the **cataloguing** and classification of materials. This is to determine where items should be housed within the library, and to store information about them in a catalogue (probably on a computer) so that they can be efficiently traced and retrieved when information is required. This is not a significant part of the work for many staff in a modern public library, as it tends to be done at the library headquarters on behalf of all the libraries in the area; or libraries may buy in a cataloguing service from a major library system supplier.

Specialist librarians could be involved in classifying and cataloguing individual collections of books, art works, music, etc, perhaps for an auction house or an insurance company.

They **compile** bibliographies – in academic libraries, a typical task is compiling lists of books and other materials on specific topics, in response to requests.

They **manage** the library, information service or resource centre, its staff, contents and systems.

They tell people about the library or information service, and **promote** its services and stock, **displaying** that stock to best effect. They **help** library users to find the book they require and **organise** an efficient reservation service for readers to reserve particular materials they want. They also **prepare** packs of relevant information on specific subjects such as bereavement, setting up a small business, etc.

Librarians in the public library and information service may be involved in **working with the community** – providing space for (and organising) exhibitions, cultural activities, meetings, talks, poetry readings, children's story sessions and other activities during school holidays. As part of their community services, public librarians look after the needs of elderly and housebound people through Books on Wheels, disabled and disadvantaged people through Talking Books for the Blind, special books for readers with learning difficulties, and large-print books for those with sight problems. They also make special provision for ethnic minorities and other special groups.

What makes a good library and information professional?

Whilst a love of books is an asset and most librarians enjoy reading, these qualities are not essential for the job. There are many other qualities which are more important.

They include:

- being able to deal with all kinds of people in a pleasant, tactful and efficient manner without getting flustered;
- having a lively interest in searching out information, whatever the format, to satisfy enquirers in all types of libraries and information services – including retrieving information from computer databases;
- being able to organise one's own work and that of the staff, to achieve efficiency;
- having a wide general knowledge, some familiarity with foreign languages, an interest in current events and a reliable memory. A good visual memory is important for the librarian of an art collection;
- being prepared to work shifts, in most public and academic libraries – not minding having to work some evenings and some Saturdays, as these are the times most convenient to many users;

- in most, but not necessarily all jobs, being reasonably fit — important in a job which may keep you on your feet;
- a high degree of professionalism.

TRAINING

Professional library and information work is an all-graduate profession. There are two main ways of training and either route is acceptable for work in the public library service. For some special and academic library posts, the second route may be preferred:

- A degree in library/information studies, taken singly or as a joint honours degree with another subject. This qualifies for a mandatory award.
- A degree in any subject followed by a full-time or part-time postgraduate course in library/information studies or information science. Bursaries and studentships for full-time postgraduate courses are very few and must be applied for through the academic institution offering the course. You should get some practical experience in a library or information-related job before a postgraduate course, particularly if applying for a bursary or studentship. Usually, nine months' to a year's work experience is required; details of some temporary positions are available from the Library Association from October to July. Degree-level qualifications are required for admission to postgraduate courses.

Minimum requirements for degree courses are usually two A levels/Advanced GNVQ/BTEC National Diploma, plus supporting GCSEs. You will need English language GCSE at grade C or equivalent; a foreign language and a science are useful.

Mature entrants may be accepted onto some degree courses without the usual entry qualifications, as previous experience and knowledge are taken into account.

There are information posts in some organisations which can be entered by graduates without professional qualifications, but your career would be limited if you were not fully qualified. Most library and information professionals belong to the Library Association, the chartered professional body in the UK. To satisfy the Library Association's criteria for admission to its professional Register of Chartered Members, most candidates will have successfully completed a degree or postgraduate course accredited by the Association, followed by a minimum of one year's approved training while in a first professional post, plus one or two years' experience prior to submitting their application.

For detailed information and a list of courses, write to the Library Association.

Library assistant

Library assistants help run libraries. Their job involves:

- issuing books and other materials to borrowers, often using a computer system;
- checking returned items and putting them back on the shelves;
- helping people to find books and information;
- sending reminders to borrowers who keep books and other materials too long;
- informing people that items they have requested have arrived;
- helping with filing and other administrative and clerical work;
- dealing with enquiries.

Library assistants can work in any type of library mentioned above, including mobile library vans. To be good at the work, you need to get on well with all sorts of people, and to be patient and not easily flustered by sudden rushes of work or difficult customers. A good memory helps, and a liking for dealing with information. 'Awkward' hours are usually entailed, with some evening/weekend work. There is often scope for part-time work.

> ### Sue – local studies librarian
>
> 'I work in the local studies section of the county library. I look after collections of old maps, photographs, tapes and videos, magazines and newspapers, books and drawings. Much of our newspaper collection is now stored on microfiche, which takes up a lot less space.
>
> I spend most of my time helping people with enquiries – children doing a school project on working canals, someone wanting information on factory working conditions in 1850, photographs needed to help with our local hospital's centenary celebrations, and usually a few people are in here to research their family tree.
>
> The rest of my time is spent keeping the materials in reasonable condition and making repairs. I also catalogue each item on to a computer database. I really enjoy acquiring new material for the collection, and sometimes people will donate items. Last year I interviewed several residents of an elderly people's home and we now have their memories of life in our town all stored on video.
>
> We are really short of space and lots of items have to be stored in the basement. It can be quite hard and dusty work at times, but I really enjoy finding out about the past.'

EDUCATION AND TRAINING

Educational requirements are usually a minimum of four GCSEs at grade C, with English being the most important subject. The basic duties are learned on-the-job, but you can also take a one-year, part-time or distance learning City & Guilds Library and Information Assistants Certificate. A Higher National Certificate on Library and Information Science is available by distance learning over two years. National Vocational Qualifications in information and library services at levels 2 to 4 are also available, but it is unlikely that NVQs will eliminate the need for a degree to achieve professional status.

Vacancies for library assistants can be found in local newspapers and, occasionally, the *Library Association Record Vacancies Supplement*, which is sent out only to members of the Association and mainly carries professional posts.

Promotion opportunities are rather limited, though there are posts for Senior Library Assistants in larger libraries. The Library Association produces an information booklet on job-hunting for members.

Adults: note that maturity and previous experience may mean that stated entry requirements can be relaxed.

EXHIBITION & CONFERENCE ORGANISING

> Organising an event like an exhibition or a conference means you need the skills of an artist, a logistics expert, a planner, a financier, travel agent, business manager, and public relations officer. There are no specific entry qualifications, but for positions with responsibility degree-level qualifications or relevant work experience will generally be asked for. It is possible for those with fewer qualifications to get started at assistant level, and work their way up.

Since the Great Exhibition of 1856 held in Crystal Palace, the idea of mounting exhibitions, to display, celebrate and sell every type of article from boats to carbon fibres, has continued to interest people.

Conferences and exhibitions are a way of:

- celebrating special events or anniversaries;
- discussing current issues;
- demonstrating new products or techniques;
- promoting a campaign;
- enhancing communications within large groups;
- improving public relations;
- bringing together practitioners in a particular trade or profession;
- promoting awareness of towns or cities.

What do organisers do?
Many exhibition and conference organisers work for an increas-

ing number of organisations who specialise in events management, within the UK and internationally. Other organisers could be employees who are asked by their own company or institution to organise a conference, or maybe produce a stand for an exhibition.

Work out the finances
This all happens well before the event takes place. The venue has to be arranged and costs agreed. Other expenses, such as hire of furniture and equipment, have to be accounted for. Exhibitors or delegates need to be contacted, and a list drawn up. Charges for exhibiting or for attending the conference or exhibition must be set. Other sources of income, generated during the conference or exhibition, need to be taken into account.

Other responsibilities could include:
- ensuring local safety and planning regulations are met;
- negotiating with the police and fire service on safety or parking issues;
- arranging proper insurance cover;
- checking that electricity and other essential services are provided;
- deciding on and booking the catering arrangements;
- organising that the right furniture and other technical equipment is provided;
- for conferences – deciding on the programme or speakers and contacting speakers;
- for exhibitions – scheduling and arranging any special demonstrations or workshops;
- planning the publicity and promotion of the event through newspapers, radio, TV, etc;
- attending to any other printed material which needs to be supplied – plans, programmes, instructions, etc.

As the specific date draws nearer, an organiser must check that everything has been done, answer a host of enquiries, and follow up any problems that may have arisen. There will be many antisocial and stressful hours to be worked, prior to the opening deadline! The job does not finish with the opening of the event either, as the organiser must be on hand to see that all runs smoothly. Afterwards, the venue must be cleared and any monitoring exercises followed up.

What does it take?
- the ability to plan and analyse;
- a good head for business and finance;
- an artistic ability;
- presentation skills;
- good communication skills;
- supervisory skills;
- problem-solving skills.

EDUCATION AND TRAINING

Getting started from school: there are no specific entry requirements for this kind of work, but employers will generally look for some qualifications, such as GCSEs, depending on the level of responsibility of the position. It can then be possible to work your way up.

Getting started after higher education: degrees in marketing, business, communications or public relations provide a useful background. To study for a degree, you need a minimum of two A levels plus supporting GCSEs, or equivalent qualifications such as an Advanced GNVQ or National Diploma. Alternatively, you could consider Higher National Diploma courses in Conference and Exhibition Management, or Arts and Events Administration. A number of colleges offer HNC/HND courses in exhibition design. For an HND you need to have studied two A levels and passed at least one (or the equivalent, such as Advanced GNVQ) – or a foundation art course if studying design.

Entry after working in other fields: marketing, public relations, journalism, advertising or business experience which has involved organising special events could all provide useful experience for people who wish to move into conference or exhibition organising.

Further training: Courses offered by the Communications, Advertising and Marketing Foundation (CAM) can be followed through part-time study or distance learning.

DISPLAY, EXHIBITION & INTERIOR DESIGN

> Display, exhibition and interior design are specialisms of three-dimensional design. These may overlap in terms of the work, techniques used, training and employment.

Display and exhibition designers know about colour, shape and form in two- and three-dimensional design, and techniques of graphics, lettering, photography and printing. **Interior designers** also have specialist knowledge connected with lighting, fabrics and furnishings, besides architectural and constructional aspects of their work. *Computer-aided design* is widely used.

Displays for shops and offices

Well-designed window and counter displays advertise a firm's goods and attract customers. Displays are changed often so that the attention of passers-by is drawn to them. Display and interior designers may work as a team with fashion designers, packaging designers and graphic artists, working on layout, fittings, lights, staff uniforms and packaging materials.

Some display work for shops and offices is done by professional designers, but, in smaller businesses, it is done by talented employees. In larger department and chain stores, a team may do all the display work in a particular region. Designers also work at the head office of an organisation, creating displays to be installed in all their branches at the same time. A uniform look from branch to branch is an important part of modern marketing. (See next section.)

Exhibition design

This includes anything from huge one-off exhibitions, like the Motor Show, to educational displays in museums and public libraries. Many different materials and techniques may be used. Designers may use ready-made display stands or design their own. There is also work for modelmakers and craftspeople in wood, acrylics and other materials used to construct exhibitions.

Many museums use independent design companies specialising

in museum work and heritage interpretation. The museum designer needs to know about museum objects and how they are perceived, as well as about conservation. All exhibition designers need skills in interpretation, the organisation of space and management of visitors.

Interior design

This involves the design of living, working and playing space inside buildings – colour schemes, materials for floors, walls and ceilings, and fixtures and fittings. Most work is concerned with industrial, commercial and public buildings, although there may be opportunities in private houses. Technical ability is needed for drawing up visual ideas and working plans, and some interior designers train first as architects.

Good communication skills are required to interpret what the client wants. For example, a hotel owner may want to follow the style of a certain period.

Interior designers may work in specialised design practices with a team including architects, or a design practice offering a wide range of services such as graphic, textile and product designs. Others may work freelance. There are also opportunities with manufacturers of furniture and furnishings, and with hotel, retailing and building companies.

Other similar specialisms

Theatre design and TV/film set design use similar skills and creative talents, but the designer must also know about lighting, special effects and costume. Some specialist training courses are available.

EDUCATION AND TRAINING

College and university courses

There are full-time college courses including BTEC National

Diploma/Advanced GNVQ, BTEC Higher National and degree courses. The British Display Society also runs its own courses. To get a place on a BDS or BTEC National/Advanced GNVQ course, you will need evidence of your ability in art, and three or four GCSEs at grade C, or an Intermediate GNVQ.

Degree/HND courses require completion of a foundation course in art and design (or other preliminary-level course) or a BTEC National Diploma/Advanced GNVQ. Students straight from an A level course may be considered. There may be exemptions from formal entry requirements for mature applicants to courses.

Private courses
There are a few private courses in interior design (more for leisure than professional purposes) and correspondence courses. The Interior Decorators and Designers Association can supply addresses, if you send them a stamped, self-addressed envelope. These courses may not, however, qualify for an LEA award or lead to a recognised qualification.

If you don't want to do a college course

Opportunities are much more limited, though if you have a flair for design, you may be able to get away without formal training. Evening classes or correspondence courses may help. It is possible to get a job as a shop assistant and then move on to the display side by showing an interest in the work. In the same way, you could get involved in the display work of other organisations – for instance, if you worked in a library or museum not big enough to have its own display designer.

Adults: note that maturity and previous experience may mean that stated entry requirements can be relaxed.

just THE JOB

THEATRE & TV WORK

> There are many jobs 'behind the scenes' in a theatre or TV production, all essential to the success of a production. These include costume, make-up, lighting and music, theatre or set design, as well as management and production. Some jobs require experience as well as academic and professional qualifications; all the areas of work require a lot of stamina and determination!

Backstage theatre work

Although directors and designers can earn good salaries when they are working, most technical jobs in the theatre are not particularly well paid. The majority of technicians rely on the large amounts of essential overtime to boost their earnings. Working hours are long and involve much evening and some night work. You will find below a short description of the jobs and some information on training, but further research on your part will be necessary to gather more detailed information. Any experience you can gain in amateur theatre productions is always useful.

The roles requiring the most detailed historical awareness and accuracy, to ensure authenticity, are those concerned with set and costume design, wardrobe, make up and 'props'.

NVQs in Stagecraft

These qualifications are now available for people already working or training backstage in the theatre or in performing arts.

They cover lighting, flying (controlling scenery and equipment from the space above the stage), costumes and scenery at NVQ levels 1 or 2, and are assessed at a few selected centres.

Director

The director puts the whole show together, combining and controlling the work of actors, writers, musicians, singers, dancers and backstage workers. The job requires creativity and organising ability.

Producer

The producer raises the money for the show, and generally ensures that it actually happens. In the commercial theatre, the producer usually starts with finding the backers for a production, followed by arranging hire of a theatre, suitable performers and a director.

Stage manager

The stage manager coordinates the work of the whole backstage team, keeping rehearsals and performances running smoothly. Because of the large team, the theatre has to be a highly disciplined place and the stage manager is the person in charge. Stage management or technical theatre courses at various levels are available at a number of drama colleges and some institutions of further and higher education.

Production manager

The production manager assists the director and producer with general backstage administration, and represents the communication link between the actors and technicians and the company management. Production managers usually have a stage management background.

Assistant stage manager

The assistant stage manager helps with jobs like getting props, playing-in taped sound effects, prompting, making tea and 10,000 other useful little tasks. ASMs would usually have done either stage management or acting training.

Set designer

The set is designed and plans are produced, with working drawings and models from which it will be made. Some set designers might also design the costumes, to achieve an integrated effect. There are theatre design courses at degree and BTEC Higher National Diploma level. See *Art & Design* in the *Just the Job!* series for details.

Costume designer

The costume designer designs and superintends the costume for the production. He/she decides whether costumes should be newly made, hired or modified from stock. The job does not usually include the practical work of sewing, but it is concerned with producing the working sketches and drawings for the wardrobe department. A designer needs to be able to research costumes of different times and places. A course in fashion design would provide a useful background. Alternatively, there are specialist courses in costume design and theatre wardrobe.

Vicky – costume archive director, Paris Opera

'My job working with theatre costumes, in Paris, sounds pretty glamorous, and of course, in some ways it is. I do get to see all the new productions and meet directors and artists and go on foreign visits to see costume archives in other countries.

My job is based in the costume store, which is out in the suburbs and not part of the huge and prestigious new Opera Bastille in the middle of Paris, so my working day starts with a long ride on the Metro. We have all the *costumes for the ballet going back for many years, so the job is partly maintaining the archive as well servicing revivals of more recent productions.*

One very interesting job I had to do recently was to research the costumes for a ballet last performed in the twenties by the Ballets Russes. All I had to work on were the reviews of the period, some black and white photographs and the memories of some very elderly dancers about colours and materials. I ended up tracking down a few of the original costumes which had survived and finished up in a collection in England.

Unlike the rather insecure nature of theatre work in the UK, I am a French civil servant, with all the advantages in terms of job security, holidays and pensions that this status involves.

I was very lucky to get started in this work. I had an art college training in England and moved to France to get married. After having a child I wanted to get back to work and did a training scheme involving costume work. A friend working with the Opera suggested I did some work experience with the company and this, very fortunately, led to a permanent job doing practical work in the costume archive. I have gradually worked my way up to my current post as my experience and knowledge have grown. Naturally I have to speak French well. I now find that my English has started to get a bit strange as I catch myself translating French expressions directly into English.

Wardrobe master/mistress
This involves making, altering and maintaining the costumes. In

a rep theatre, the job also involves looking after the costume store, which can be quite large. The work can be very pressured, with deadlines which must be met. Practical skills are very important, particularly the ability to translate drawings into a finished product. A good knowledge of materials is required. There are full-time BTEC HND and degree courses, BTEC National and college diploma courses at many theatre schools.

Wardrobe assistant

Wardrobe assistants help with the routine sewing, ironing and cleaning of costumes. A wardrobe assistant must have good practical skills and be quick and flexible.

Dresser

The dresser looks after wigs and costumes, helps actors dress for the performance and generally assists them. A dresser could combine this job with being a wardrobe assistant. Dressers are not necessarily trained, but wardrobe masters/mistresses often are.

Properties

The properties manager makes sure that all the 'props' – looking as authentic and historically accurate as possible – are there for the performance and put back at the end of the show. During rehearsals, all the necessary items are bought, borrowed or made and, during the run, are repaired or replaced as necessary. There are courses in property-making at various drama and further education colleges, up to degree level.

Make-up

In theatre, actors generally do their own make-up, so opportunities for make-up assistants may be few and far between. However, make-up artists, working in the theatre in another capacity, may be called upon for advice. There are more opportunities in television and film (see below). Several FE colleges offer diploma courses in theatrical make-up, or it may be included as an option in more general beauty and make-up courses.

Stagehand

The stagehand moves all the items on the stage which are not properties (props) or electrics. Furniture and chunks of scenery are their responsibility, but *not* anything the actors carry – fans, teacups, revolvers and so forth. A theatre will have a small group of resident stagehands and will take on extra staff when needed. This is an area of work where it is possible to get a foot in the door.

Scene painter

Scene painters work with the set designer and the carpenter producing the set. Scene painting is a rather specialised job, a craft rather than a creative process. RADA offers a diploma course.

Carpenter

The carpenter works in a workshop and on stage, making new sets and modifying and repairing old ones. Practical ability, with a strong interest in the theatre, is essential. It is not always necessary to be a skilled joiner or qualified carpenter. There is a full-time diploma course at RADA.

Other backstage roles in theatre include electrician, lighting designer and technician, musical director and arranger, repetiteur/rehearsal pianist and choreographer – see *Leisure, Sport & Entertainment* in the *Just the Job!* series.

TV support work
Set designer
Set designers and assistants are a vital part of the production team, as their work has to reflect the ideas of the producer/director. Trainees are normally recruited from students who have taken a relevant design course.

Properties, or props, include portable items like furnishings, crockery, books or equipment used on set to bring a scene to life. They may be bought, hired or made by people working closely with the set and costume teams. Historical accuracy is very important.

Costume designer and assistant
For this work a very high standard of creative ability is needed, together with a good knowledge of historical costume. There are relevant design courses at BTEC Higher National diploma or degree level at a limited number of colleges.

Costume department and dresser
Competent and experienced dressmakers who can work fast are needed. Successful applicants have often had experience in theatrical costumiers or repertory theatres. Sometimes costumes and accessories are hired rather than specially made, and a budget has to be kept to. **Dressers** need to be mature and able to deal with all sorts of people.

Dressmaker
An appropriate qualification such as City & Guilds dressmaking is usually required, combined with two years' experience in a theatrical costumiers.

Make-up assistant
Television performers are made-up by trained staff. For a career as a make-up artist, you need to be a mature person with a good

general educational background, and with a hairdressing or make-up qualification, or, ideally, both. A level qualifications (or their equivalent) in art and English are an asset. An interest in, and experience of, stage make-up is very useful.

As an alternative to ordinary hairdressing or beauty experience, there are suitable courses at further education colleges (as well as many private courses), specialising in theatre, television and film make-up, hair-styling and wig-dressing. The *Directory of Further Education* has course details.

Much TV make-up work is concerned with preparing people for interviews, documentaries, chat shows and light entertainment, and only a small part of the work involves special effects for period dramas, 'horror' make-ups, etc.

TRAINING OPPORTUNITIES

All jobs and training opportunities in support work for broadcasting are advertised in the national press and on Ceefax. Independent television companies and the BBC have a similar range of jobs, sometimes with slightly different titles. In looking for training opportunities, it is necessary (but also worthwhile) to write to individual companies – see Further Information section.

Skillset, the training organisation for the broadcasting and film industry, is overseeing the introduction of NVQs and Modern Apprenticeships in many areas, including crafts.

just THE JOB

HOROLOGIST

> Horology is the making and repairing of clocks. The skills needed to work with both traditional mechanics and new digital technology make up the job of the horologist. A good general education is needed, but no specific entry qualifications.
>
> Horology is a very specialised science. It involves miniaturised engineering, so good eyesight is essential.

There are times when we need very precise timing, down to hundredths of a second — perhaps to time a downhill skier or launch a space vehicle. Horologists need to use miniaturised mechanical engineering to service such complex and astonishingly accurate timepieces, and must learn how to use electronic diagnostic equipment. Even miniaturised mechanical engineering is giving way to microscopic quartz-controlled integrated circuitry, as new technologies continue to be developed.

At the same time, the traditional skills are still in demand. Antique clocks go up in value all the time, and they often need to be repaired or restored. Horologists need to know the theory and practical applications of electricity, electronics, mechanics and other branches of physics. Although there's scope to specialise, horologists should be familiar with both old and new timepieces. You might have to make or restore parts for antique clocks, and also master the completely different skills needed to repair modern mechanical, electrical and electronic clocks and watches. It is said that you should be able to make a clock from scratch to be able to repair one!

EDUCATION AND TRAINING

The British Horological Institute was founded over 130 years ago to educate and train watch and clockmakers. Of course, the BHI training programmes have been kept up to date, and are being revised all the time! There are various ways of training currently available.

Correspondence courses – the BHI runs a three-part correspondence course which prepares students for the preliminary, intermediate and final grade examinations.

Full-time and day release courses in technical horology are available at some higher education institutions. These courses lead to the final grade BHI exams. Applicants should have had a good general education in English, maths, physics and design and technology. Good eyesight is essential and, of course, applicants must have a genuine interest in horology. There are no upper age limits. These courses qualify for discretionary awards only, which are in short supply, so apply in good time.

There are also college courses available for people with disabilities. Further details of all the courses can be obtained from the British Horological Institute.

Evening courses are available in one or two areas – see the CRAC *Directory of Further Education*.

Short courses – besides courses in state colleges, there are various short courses available in the private sector, including some courses of an 'activity holiday' type. These might be especially suited to adults thinking about a change of career and wishing to try out their interest. The BHI runs seminars on various specialist subjects.

Advanced courses – on completing a two-year full-time course, students are able to continue their studies at advanced level on a part-time day basis. Students doing this attend the college for one day per week, studying advanced clockmaking and adjusting techniques, and processes such as gilding, plating and engraving and management and salesmanship. For people with some experience, there are also specialist courses in the restoration of antique clocks and timepieces.

Adults may be able to find a government-sponsored training scheme – ask at the Jobcentre. Horology is certainly a very suitable career for mature entry, especially as self-employment is one of the main work options.

PROSPECTS

Some students are sponsored for their training by firms who give full-time employment when the training period is completed. Others find work with jewellers, government departments, museums, instrument firms, etc. A chain of jewellers' shops may employ more than twenty watch and clock repairers. Of course, self-employment is also an option. You could take on any work going, or act as a local agent for a particular manufacturer.

Prospects in horology are very good. Besides opportunities in horology, it is also possible for qualified people to work in jobs such as instrument adjustment, surgical instrument manufacture and repair, since the skills needed are very similar.

FOR FURTHER INFORMATION

GENERAL
Historical Association – 59a Kennington Park Road, London SE11 4JH. Tel: 0171 735 3901. Can supply the leaflet *Why study history? History and choosing your career.*

Working in History, published by COIC.

ARCHAEOLOGY
CADW – Crown Building, Cathays Park, Cardiff CF1 3NQ. Tel: 01222 500200. (The Welsh ancient monuments organisation.)

Council for British Archaeology – Bowes-Morrell House, 111 Walmgate, York YO1 2UA. Tel: 01904 671417. May be able to help with specific queries from volunteers seeking suitable excavations to work on and general education/careers enquiries.

English Heritage – 23 Savile Row, London W1X 1AB. Tel: 0171 973 3000.

Historic Scotland – Longmore House, Salisbury Place, Edinburgh EH9 1SH. Tel: 0131 668 8600.

Institute of Archaeology – University College, 31–34 Gordon Square, London WC1H 0PY. Tel: 0171 387 7050. Publishes a list of overseas excavations.

Institute of Field Archaeologists – University of Manchester, Oxford Road, Manchester M13 9PL. Tel: 0161 275 2304. Provides a job information service and bulletin for qualified archaeologists.

Ironbridge Institute – Ironbridge Gorge Museum, Ironbridge, Telford, Shropshire TF8 7AW. Tel: 01952 432751. (Of particular interest to industrial archaeologists.)

Young Archaeologists' Club – for 9–16-year-olds. Same address as the Council for British Archaeology.

Working in Archaeology, a factsheet from the Institute of Field Archaeologists.
The British Archaeology Year Book, includes details of degree and postgraduate courses – available from the Council for British Archaeology.
British Archaeology, published by the Council for British Archaeology – by annual subscription. Incorporates *CBA Briefing*, which lists all excavations looking for helpers.
Current Archaeology, a quarterly, available on subscription from 9 Nassington Road, London NW3 2TX. Tel: 0171 435 7517.

ARCHIVES
Society of Archivists – Information House, 20–24 Old Street, London EC1V 9AP. Tel: 0171 253 5087.

Heritage management and museum work – an AGCAS graduate careers information booklet, available in careers libraries or from CSU, Armstrong House, Oxford Road, Manchester M1 7ED. Tel: 0161 236 9816, ext 250/251.
Archives as a Career is available from the Society of Archivists.
Record Repositories in Great Britain, published by HMSO, gives addresses of record offices and is available in reference libraries.

You could also contact your local authority records office.

HERALDRY & GENEALOGY
Association of Genealogists and Record Agents – 29 Badgers Close, Horsham RH12 5RU.
The College of Arms – Queen Victoria Street, London EC4V 4BT. Tel: 0171 248 2762.
Federation of Family History Societies – The Administrator, The Benson Room, Birmingham and Midland Institute, Margaret Street, Birmingham B3 3BS.
The Heraldry Society – 44–45 Museum Street, London WC1A 1LY. Tel: 0171 430 2172.
Institute of Heraldic and Genealogical Studies – 79/82 Northgate, Canterbury CT1 1BA. Tel: 01227 768664.

Society of Genealogists – 14 Charterhouse Buildings, Goswell Road, London EC1M 7BA. Tel: 0171 251 8799.

Genealogists' Magazine, published by the Society of Genealogists.
Family History News and Digest, published by the Federation of Family History Societies.

HERITAGE JOBS
CADW – Crown Building, Cathays Park, Cardiff CF1 3NQ. Tel: 01222 500200. (The Welsh ancient monuments organisation.)
English Heritage – 23 Savile Row, London W1X 1AB. Tel: 0171 973 3000.
Guild of Registered Tourist Guides – The Guild House, 52D Borough High Street, London SE1 1XN. Tel: 0171 403 1115.
Historic Scotland – Longmore House, Salisbury Place, Edinburgh EH9 1SH. Tel: 0131 668 8600.
International Institute for Conservation of Historic and Artistic Works – 6 Buckingham Street, London WC2N 6BA. Tel: 0171 839 5975.
National Monuments Record Centre (NMRC) – Kemble Drive, Swindon SN2 2GZ. Tel: 01793 414600.
The National Trust – 36 Queen Anne's Gate, London SW1H 9AS. Tel: 0171 222 9251.
The National Trust for Scotland – 5 Charlotte Square, Edinburgh EH2 4DU. Tel: 0131 226 5922.
Northern Ireland Environment and Heritage Service – 5/33 Hill Street, Belfast BT1 2LA. Tel: 012332 235000.
Royal Commission on Ancient and Historic Monuments of Scotland – John Sinclair House, 16 Bernard Terrace, Edinburgh EH8 9NX. Tel: 0131 662 1456.

Heritage management and museum work, an AGCAS careers information leaflet, available in careers libraries or from CSU, Armstrong House, Oxford Road, Manchester M1 7ED. Tel: 0161 236 9816, ext 250/251.

MUSEUMS & ART GALLERIES

Association of Independent Museums – c/o London Transport Museum, 39 Wellington Street, Covent Garden, London WC2E 7BB. Tel: 0171 379 6344.

Department of Museum Studies – University of Leicester, 105 Princess Road East, Leicester LEI 7LG. Tel: 0116 2523 962 for postgraduate information.

International Institute for the Conservation of Historic and Artistic Works – 6 Buckingham Street, London WC2N 6BA. Tel: 0171 839 5975.

Museums Association – 42 Clerkenwell Close, London EC1R 0PA. Tel: 0171 608 2933.

Museums and Galleries Commission – 16 Queen Anne's Gate, London SW1H 9AA. Tel: 0171 233 4200.

Museum Training Institute – 1st Floor, Glyde House, Glydegate, Bradford BD5 0UP. Tel: 01274 391056.

Training and Working in Conservation, available from the Conservation Unit of the Museum & Galleries Commission.

Museums Journal and *Museums Yearbook* can be obtained from the Museums Association (above).

Careers in Museums, available from the Museums Training Institute at the above address, also covers work in public art galleries.

Visual Arts and *Heritage Management and Museum Work* are two graduate careers information booklets published by CSU, Armstrong House, Oxford Road, Manchester M1 7ED. Tel: 0161 236 9816, ext 250/251.

CAREERS IN ANTIQUES

For details of courses available, see further and higher education handbooks, such as *Directory of Further Education* published annually by CRAC, or the *Compendium of Higher Education*.

Antiquarian Booksellers Association – Sackville House, 40 Piccadilly, London W1V 9PA. Tel: 0171 439 3118.

British Antique Dealers Association – 20 Rutland Gate, London SW7 1BD. Tel: 0171 589 4128. (List of members available – enclose a stamped, addressed envelope.)

ISVA – The Incorporated Society of Valuers and Auctioneers – Education Office, 3 Cadogan Gate, London SW1X 0AS. Tel: 0171 235 2282.

RESTORATION OF WORKS OF ART

Association of British Picture Restorers – Station Avenue, Kew, Surrey TW9 3QA. Tel: 0181 948 5644. Jan Robinson, at the Association, may be able to help with finding apprenticeships.

Conservation Unit – Museums and Galleries Commission, 16 Queen Anne's Gate, London SW1H 9AA. Tel: 0171 233 4200. Publishes two booklets: *Training in Conservation* and *Working in Conservation*.

International Centre for the Study of the Preservation and the Restoration of Cultural Property (ICCROM) – Via di San Michele 13, 00153 Roma, Italy. An international directory of courses in conservation, published by ICCROM and the Getty Conservation Institute, is available from IIC, 6 Buckingham Street, London WC2N 6BA.

Museum Training Institute – 1st Floor, Glyde House, Glydegate, Bradford BD5 0UP. Tel: 01274 391056.

United Kingdom Institute for Conservation – 6 Whitehorse Mews, 37–39 Westminster Bridge Road, London SE1 7QD. Tel: 0171 620 3371.

WORKING IN LIBRARIES & INFORMATION SERVICES

The Library Association – Information Services, 7 Ridgmount Street, London WC1E 7AE. Tel: 0171 636 7543 – publishes free careers information on where to study in the UK, financial assistance for study, qualifications for library assistants and graduate training opportunities.

CONFERENCE & EXHIBITION ORGANISING

Association of Exhibition Organisers – 26 Chapter Street, London SW1P 4ND. Tel: 0171 932 0252. Publishes a leaflet *Career Opportunities in Exhibition Organising*.

CAM Foundation – Abford House, 15 Wilton Road, London SW1V 1NJ. Tel: 0171 828 7506.

Exhibition Management is a useful bi-monthly newspaper published by FMJ International Publications Ltd., Queensway House, 2 Queensway, Redhill, Surrey RH1 1QS. Tel: 01737 768611.

Exhibition Bulletin, a directory which lists exhibition organising companies. Contact the Association of Exhibition Organisers for further details.

DISPLAY, EXHIBITION & INTERIOR DESIGN

British Display Society – 70a Crayford High Street, Dartford, Kent DA1 4EF. Tel: 01322 555755.

Chartered Society of Designers – First floor, 32–38 Saffron Hill, London EC1N 8FH. Tel: 0171 831 9777.

Interior Decorators and Designers Association – 1–4 Chelsea Harbour Design Centre, Lots Road, London SW10 0XE. Tel: 0171 349 0800.

Art and Design Courses, published by Trotman for the Design Council.

Creative Futures, available from the National Society for Education in Art, Craft and Design, The Gatehouse, Corsham Court, Corsham, Wiltshire SN13 0BZ. Tel: 01249 714825.

BACKSTAGE THEATRE WORK

Arts Council of England – Drama Department, 14 Great Peter Street, London SW1P 3NQ. Tel: 0171 333 0100.

Arts and Entertainment Training Council (AETC) – in the process of merging with AETTI (Arts and Entertainment Technicians Training Initiative) – Glyde House, Glydegate, Bradford BD5 0BQ. Tel: 01274 738800.

Association of British Theatre Technicians – 47 Bermondsey Street, London SE1 3XT. Tel: 0171 403 3778.

BECTU (Broadcasting, Entertainment, Cinematograph and Theatre Union) – 111 Wardour Street, London W1V 4AY. Tel: 0171 437 8506. The trade union for backstage and support workers in the theatre.

Spotlight – 7 Leicester Place, London WC2H 7BP. Tel: 0171 437 7631. Publishes *Contacts*, an annual list of information on production companies, agents, schools and everything to do with theatre work.

Stage Management Association – Southbank House, Black Prince Road, London SE1 7SJ. Tel: 0171 587 1514.

The Stage is a weekly newspaper, available from your newsagent or on subscription from 47 Bermondsey Street, London SE1 3XT. Tel: 0171 403 1818.

British Theatre Directory is a useful, annually updated source of theatre-related information available from Richmond House Publishing Company, Douglas House, 3 Richmond Building, London W1V 5AE. Tel: 0171 437 9556. This volume may be held in your local library.

The Association of British Theatre Technicians can send a free leaflet *So you want to work in the theatre?* on receipt of a stamped, addressed C5 envelope.

TV SUPPORT SERVICES

BBC Corporate Recruitment Services – PO Box 7000, London W5 2WY.

Broadcasting, Entertainment, Cinematograph and Theatre Union (BECTU) – 111 Wardour Street, London W1V 4AY. Tel: 0171 437 8506.

Skillset – 124 Horseferry Road, London SW1P 2TX. Tel: 0171 306 8585. (Send large stamped, addressed envelope for careers information pack.)

Independent TV companies:

Anglia Television – Anglia House, Norwich NR1 3JG. Tel: 01603 615151.

Border Television – The Broadcasting Centre, Durranhill, Carlisle CA1 3NT. Tel: 01228 25101.

Carlton Broadcasting Ltd – 101 St. Martin's Lane, London WC2N 4AZ. Tel: 0171 240 4000.

Central Broadcasting Ltd – Central House, Broad Street, Birmingham B1 2JP. Tel: 0121 643 9898.

Channel Television Ltd – The Television Centre, St Helier, Jersey, Channel Islands JE2 3ZD. Tel: 01534 68999.

Grampian Television plc – Queen's Cross, Aberdeen, AB9 2XJ. Tel: 01224 646464.

Granada Television – Granada Television Centre, Quay Street, Manchester M60 9EA. Tel: 0161 832 7211.

HTV Wales – Television Centre, Culverhouse Cross, Cardiff, CF5 6XJ. Tel: 01222 590590.

HTV West – The Television Centre, Bath Road, Bristol, BS4 3HG. Tel: 0117 977 8366.

London Weekend Television (LWT) – Television Centre, Upper Ground, London SE1 9LT. Tel: 0171 620 1620.

Scottish Television plc – Cowcaddens, Glasgow, G2 3PR. Tel: 0141 300 3000.

Tyne Tees Television – The Television Centre, City Road, Newcastle upon Tyne, NE1 2AL. Tel: 0191 261 0181.

Ulster TV – Havelock House, Ormeau Road, Belfast BT7 1EB. Tel: 01232 328122.

Westcountry Television Ltd – Western Wood Way, Langage Science Park, Plymouth PL7 5BG. Tel: 01752 333333.

Yorkshire Television – The Television Centre, Leeds LS3 1JS. Tel: 0113 243 8283.

Channel 4 Television Corporation – 124 Horseferry Road, London SW1P 2TX. Tel: 0171 396 4444.

S4C – Welsh Fourth Channel, Parc Ty Glas, Llanishen, Cardiff, CF4 5DU. Tel: 01222 747444.

BSkyB (British Sky Broadcasting) – 6 Centaurs Business Park, Grant Way, Isleworth, Middlesex, TW7 5QD. Tel: 0171 705 3000.

Independent Television News (ITN) – 200 Gray's Inn Road, London WC1X 8XZ. Tel: 0171 833 3000.

Education, Work & Training in Film, TV and Broadcasting, published by BKSTS – The Moving Image Society – 67–71 Victoria House, Vernon Place, London WC1B 4DA. Tel: 0171 242 8400.

Careers in Television and Radio, published by Kogan Page.

How to get into the Film and TV Business, published by Alma House, 22 Margaretta Terrace, London SW3 5NU.

HOROLOGY

British Horological Institute – Upton Hall, Upton, Newark, Nottinghamshire NG23 5TE. Tel: 01636 813795.